How *The Zoo Story* Became a Two-Act Play

How did *The Zoo Story* become a two-act play? It's really very simple: it always had been; I just hadn't told myself. When I wrote *The Zoo Story* in 1958 it was my first play, so to speak. Oh, I'd made a few attempts—including an embarrassing two-act play in rhymed couplets—but nothing pleased me. No, I must be fair—it was junk, all of it.

The Zoo Story seemed to me to be a much better piece—in fact, the first I felt had any individuality and merit. It would seem I was right. It has gone on to have—at this writing—49 years of frequent performance and general acceptance.

And . . . I thought it was fine, though it nagged me just a bit that it seemed to be not quite a two-character play—Jerry being so much longer a role—but more a one-and-a-half-character one. But the play "worked," so why worry?

Six years ago, however, I said to myself, "There's a first act here somewhere which will flesh out Peter fully and make the subsequent balance better."

Almost before I knew it, *Homelife* fell from my mind to the page . . . *intact*. There was the Peter I had always known—a full three-dimensional person and—wow!—here was Ann, his wife, whom I must have imagined deep down, forty-some years ago, but hadn't brought to consciousness.

So . . . here it is—the entire play as I'm sure I must have conceived it all that time past. Enjoy.

—EDWARD ALBEE
New York City, 2007

AT HOME AT THE ZOO received its world premiere by Hartford Stage Company (Michael Wilson, Artistic Director; Chris Baker, Associate Artistic Director; James D. Ireland, Managing Director), opening on June 6, 2004. It was directed by Pam MacKinnon; the set design was by Jeff Cowie; the costume design was by Jess Goldstein; the lighting design was by Howell Binkley; the assistant director was Kanthe Tabor; the assistant lighting designer was Rob White; the production stage manager was Carmelita Becnel; the assistant stage manager was Melissa Spengler; and the production manager was Deb Vandergrift. The cast was as follows:

ANN   Johanna Day
PETER   Frank Wood
JERRY   Frederick Weller

AT HOME AT THE ZOO was produced by Second Stage Theatre (Carole Rothman, Artistic Director; Ellen Richard, Executive Director; Christopher Burney, Associate Artistic Director) in New York City, opening on November 11, 2007. It was directed by Pam MacKinnon; the set design was by Neil Patel; the costume design was by Theresa Squire; the lighting design was by Kevin Adams; the assistant set designer was Lara Fabian; the assistant costume designer was Jessica Wegener; the production stage manager was C.A. Clark; the stage manager was Annette Verga-Lagier; and the production manager was Jeff Wild. The cast was as follows:

ANN   Johanna Day
PETER   Bill Pullman
JERRY   Dallas Roberts

ACT ONE—HOMELIFE

CHARACTERS

PETER: 45. Bland; not heavy; pleasant, if uninteresting looking. Tidy; circumspect. Wears glasses to read.
ANN: 38; his wife. Tall, a bit angular; pleasant-looking, unexceptional.

PLACE

Their living room; New York City, East Side, Seventies. Pleasant; a little Danish-modernish, maybe. Exit to the apartment off hallway stage-right. Exit to kitchen off hallway stage-left-ish.

TIME

One P.M. A Sunday.

ACT TWO—THE ZOO STORY

CHARACTERS

PETER: As above.
JERRY: Late thirties; not poorly dressed, but carelessly. What was once a trim and lightly muscled body has begun to go to fat; and while he is no longer handsome, it is evident that he once was. His fall from physical grace should not suggest debauchery; he has, to come closest to it, a great weariness.

PLACE

Central Park, New York City. There are two park benches. Behind them: foliage, trees, sky.

TIME

Later that same Sunday.

ACT ONE
HOMELIFE

PETER *alone, reading, a book, a textbook probably. He is absorbed; turns a page, frowns, turns back, rereads something, turns forward again. Repeats this.* ANN *comes in from the hall to the kitchen, a towel in her hand. No rush. Intention non-evident. She comes up behind* PETER—*not too close. He does not notice her.*

ANN

We should talk.
(Waits; no reply; turns, exits whence.)

PETER

(After she goes—recognizing he had heard her.)
What? We should—what?
(Louder.)
We should what?!

ANN *(Offstage.)*

What?
(Reentering.)
We should *what?*

PETER

We should *what?*

ANN

Oh.
(Slight pause.)
We should talk.
(Wipes her hands with the towel.)

PETER *(Indicates book.)*

I was reading. I'm sorry.

ANN *(Bemused.)*

It happens so often.

PETER *(A little defensive.)*

Sorry.

ANN

No; that's not what I meant.

PETER *(Confused.)*

What!

ANN

You read so . . . you get so involved—reading—more all the time.

PETER *(Smiles.)*

"Deepening concentration." Deepened concentration. Work.

ANN *(Recalling.)*

Once I talked to you for . . . it seemed *minutes* . . . about—oh, what?—the fireplace, I think, and you didn't hear a word. You were reading.

PETER *(A little unhappy.)*

The ears turn off—out, rather.

(Tiny pause.)

The fireplace? Really?

ANN

The andirons.

PETER

What was wrong? With *them*—with the andirons.

ANN *(Shrugs; stays standing.)*

Nothing really. I was wondering if I should clean them; if I should wash them.

PETER *(Book down.)*

Why?

ANN

What.

PETER

Why you should wash them.

ANN

Well, I'd noticed the fire'd made them all grey and sort of matte, and I wondered if we liked that.

PETER

Had we? *Liked* that?

ANN *(Moving to something.)*

I don't know; we never had the conversation; you never heard me; we never talked about it.

PETER *(Brow furrows a little.)*

What did you do—about the andirons?

ANN

I scrubbed them.

PETER *(Tiny pause.)*

Ah.

ANN

And then they got all matte again—all grey.

PETER

(Reaches for her hand.)

I'm sorry; I get so . . .

ANN *(Nice.)*

It doesn't *matter.*

PETER

. . . involved. I guess it goes faster that way. What are you doing with the towel?

ANN

(Looks at it; realizes something.)

Oh!

(Exits.)

PETER

(Not realizing she's gone; indicates book.)

When it's very important and very boring—like this—well, you've seen me go into like a trance? That way I don't get to think "this is so boring I can't do it." It's im*por*tant. It's probably the most important boring book we've ever done.

(Thinks.)

Well . . . *maybe.* It's hard to tell; there are so many—so important, so boring.

(Sees she's gone.)

Where *are* you? Ann?

ANN

(Reemerges, without towel.)

That was close.

PETER

What was?

ANN

Hard-boiled spinach.

PETER

Really? Can you *do* that?

ANN *(Shakes her head.)*

We'll never know. "If you're going to cook, stay with the stove"—at least in the same room.

PETER

Or microwave.

ANN

I've decided I don't *like* microwaves. It's hard to get in there and
. . . stir around; you have to trust what you're doing.

PETER

Can't you . . . stop the thing and open it up and . . .

ANN

Yes, of course you can, but it seems like cheating.

PETER

Why do we have two of them?

ANN *(Sudden, bright laugh.)*

We have two of everything.

PETER *(Pause.)*

We do?

ANN

One for the kids.

PETER

Do *they* use the microwave?

ANN *(Laughs.)*

Where do you *live?* Have you never *been* in the kitchen?

PETER *(False deliberation.)*

Uh . . . twice as I remember.

ANN

Of *course* they use the microwave—all the time.

PETER

I guess I'm the only one who doesn't.

ANN

Well, I doubt the cats do, though they *are bright.*

PETER *(Wistful.)*

I want a dog.

ANN *(Fact.)*

No you don't.

PETER *(Fact.)*

No I don't.

ANN

What's the book?

PETER *(A kind of litany.)*
It's the most boring book we've ever published.

ANN *(Delighted.)*
Really! What an advertising gimmick . . . "the most boring book
we've ever published and you know our reputation!"

PETER
. . . *and* probably the most important.

ANN *(An echo.)*
. . . *"and* probably the most important."

PETER
As textbooks go it'll most likely make us rich—the company,
anyway.

ANN

What's it about?

PETER *(Shaking his head.)*
You really don't want to know.

ANN *(Smiles; persists.)*
What's it *about?*

PETER *(Looks.)*
About seven hundred pages. I can barely *lift* it much less read
it, but I do have to read it, so . . .
    (Shrugs.)

ANN

Before I married you my mother said to me, "Why *ever* would
you want to marry a man publishes textbooks?"

PETER *(Smiles.)*

She did not.

ANN

Well, she could have, and maybe she did. "Why ever would you
want to marry a man publishes textbooks?" "Gee, Ma, *I* don't
know—seems like fun."

PETER

I thought your family liked me.

ANN

They *do*. "He's a good, solid man," Dad said. I've told you this.
"None of this . . . fly-by-night fiction stuff."

PETER *(Laughs.)*

"Fly-by-night." What does that *mean?* Bats? And how does it
relate to fiction?

ANN

I made it up. He never said it. Look it up.

PETER

What?

ANN

Fly-by-night.

PETER

Hmmm. Maybe I will.

ANN

Or have one of your researchers do it. Is it really that boring?
"The most boring etc.?"

PETER *(Thinks; concludes.)*
Yes; except maybe Trollope's *Autobiography—which* we didn't
publish, naturally.

ANN
I never read it.

PETER
Very few have . . . all the way through. I tried: it kept falling out
of my hands.
    (Reconsiders.)
Well . . . slipping.

ANN *(Pats him.)*
This is your party thing; this Trollope thing; you do this at parties.

PETER *(Genuine.)*
I do?!

ANN
Lots.

PETER
I didn't *know!*

ANN
Doesn't matter. Makes you look smart and funny, which you are
*any*way.

PETER *(Embarrassed.)*
I'm *sorry.*

ANN
It's a *good* one! Keep it; it's a keeper.

PETER *(A little sarcastic.)*
Thanks!
    (Moving on.)
*Any*way, next time you have trouble falling asleep—*try* it.
    (Lifts the book.)
Or this.

ANN

Thanks.

(*Ironic.*)

If I ever have trouble sleeping.

PETER (*Pause.*)

Hm? What?

ANN

If I ever have trouble sleeping—she said ironically.

PETER (*Slight pause.*)

I see you, leaving bed—before dawn—when you think I'm asleep.

ANN

Do you?

PETER

Yes. Why?

ANN

Don't you ever worry? You don't say "Why can't you sleep? Where are you going? What is it you want?"

PETER

You come *back;* I assume you're . . . about your business.

ANN (*Small smile.*)

My nighttime business. My pre-dawn business.

PETER

I'm *sorry;* perhaps . . .

ANN (*Not accusatory.*)

For all *you* know I could go out in my nightdress, down in the elevator, out the door, down Seventy-fourth Street, to the corner; stand there; scream.

PETER *(Reasonable.)*

You could: yes; but you wouldn't.

ANN

. . . or *get* there, strip off completely, lie down, spread my legs to the night—the pre-dawn.

    (Pause.)

No, I *wouldn't, would* I.

PETER *(Smiles.)*

No; you wouldn't.

ANN

Some night, get up; follow me. You've never done it? Followed me?

PETER

No.

ANN

All these years?

PETER

No; it's something people do—get up.

ANN

Who are all these people? People you've slept with?

PETER

No! It's what people *do*. Where do you go?

ANN

Some night, get up; follow me. To the kitchen, usually; a cup of tea.

    (Dreamy.)

One night I sat for an hour . . . and I thought about having my breasts cut off.

PETER

Where!?

ANN

In the kitchen.

PETER *(Puts book down; laughs.)*

You didn't!

ANN

No? Over twenty percent of us get breast cancer, and over fifty percent of those of us do die of it. What better way to avoid it if you're young enough.

PETER

Are you?

ANN

I don't *know.* Probably. Probably *not.*

PETER *(A little hurt.)*

You would *tell* me, wouldn't you?

ANN

What?

PETER

If you were thinking of it . . . seriously.

ANN *(You imbecile!)*

No! I'd go to some clinic where they do that sort of thing on the fly—or the fly-by-night—and I'd go in and I'd say "Hello, I'd like to have my breasts cut off, please, prophylactic, and all, and don't tell my hubby."

PETER *(A little embarrassed.)*

Do you think there *are* women do that?

ANN *(Very matter of fact.)*

There are women do anything.

PETER

Everything?

ANN

Either; both.

PETER

You were really *thinking* of doing that?

ANN

I was thinking about thinking about it—about what it would be like to think about it, about doing it.

PETER

Ah.

ANN

Once you hear of an idea you never know where it will lodge itself, when it will move from something learned to something . . . *consid*erable, something you *might* think about, which is not far from *being* thought about, if you wanted to, or *needed* to.

PETER *(A sad truth.)*

We all die of *some*thing.

ANN

Sooner or later.

PETER

Yes, but . . .

ANN

Yes, but! Oh, you *do* love pedantry so . . . dying of *not* doing something can be carelessness!

PETER *(Appalled.)*

Having your breasts cut off can be called *care*?!

ANN *(Thinks about it.)*

An extreme case; yes.

PETER

Only a crazy person.

ANN

Then there are lots of loonies around.

PETER

No one.

ANN *(Slowly; articulated.)*

Ma . . . ny.

PETER

Only a crazy person.

ANN *(Shrugs.)*

Have it your way.

(Laughs; a sudden remembering.)

I remember the night I thought about thinking about it. My mother had called me that day and told me she's decided to have an affair with somebody.

PETER

(Not displeased; maybe just happy to be on another subject.)

She *did?!* Who?!

ANN

I don't know—somebody.

PETER

Yes, but you said . . .

ANN

I said she told me—why are we moving this conversation away from me, by the way, away from something that concerns *me?*— that she'd decided to have an affair with somebody.

PETER

Yes!

ANN

And of course I asked *who*—who are you going to have this affair *with?*

PETER

Of course.

ANN

Not necessarily. I might not have wanted to pry—or to know.

PETER

Yes, that's possible.

ANN

But I *did:* I *did* want to pry or know . . . and so I did.

PETER *(Shy.)*

Pry?

ANN

Ask. Who are you going to have an affair *with,* I said—casual-like. Hm?

PETER

And . . . ?

ANN

And she said she didn't know; she hadn't decided, or maybe she hadn't met the person.

PETER

The man.

ANN

Not *necessarily.* All she knew was that she'd decided to have an affair with somebody. She didn't know *who.*

PETER

It just seemed like a good idea?!

ANN

Yes; or so she thought. "Does it seem like a good idea?" I asked her. "I assume it does." "Well, not necessarily," she said. "It might be something *bad* I want—of course for reasons I haven't figured out yet." "You get more complex with age," I told her. "Like cheese," she smiled. I think. "Something bad might be a good idea in that case," I said. "Yes," she said. "Isn't life odd."

PETER

Like hacking off your breasts.

ANN

Having them hacked off.

PETER

Yes; sorry.

ANN

We're back on *that,* are we?

PETER

Well, it's—did her telling you lead you to your breast thing, in some weird, convoluted female way? Her telling you about wanting to have an affair lead you to contemplating having your . . . ?

ANN

"Weird, convoluted female way?" Who *are* you?

PETER

Sorry. *Did* it?

ANN

What, lead me to contemplating it? No, I don't think so. Though maybe. Maybe if I had no breasts the likelihood of having an affair—if I were planning to have one—would be . . . well, I was going to say diminished.

PETER

Why not! Why *not* say diminished?

ANN

Well; probably; yes, though there *are* people around . . .

PETER

. . . who like that sort of thing?—lack of thing, of something?
    (Feels his own.)
"Breastlessness?!"

ANN *(Chuckles.)*

There are people like everything—anything.

(Peter chuckles, too.)

PETER

Symmetry! God, I love symmetry.

(Serious.)

Are you . . . planning something?

ANN

You mean beyond dinner? Beyond feeding the cats—and the rest of the menagerie?

PETER

Yes.

ANN

Beyond *thinking* about thinking about something?

PETER

Yes.

ANN *(Shrugs.)*

Oh, *I* don't know. Like what? Like having an affair—like mother like daughter? I hope not. I hope I'm not thinking about that.

PETER *(Shy.)*

Me, too.

ANN

You, too, what? You hope *I'm* not, or you hope *you're* not?

PETER *(Sad smile.)*

Either; both.

ANN *(Straight.)*

Me, too.

(Pause.)

The nights *are* strange—you asleep; I *look* at you—unconscious, lost to the world, as they say.

PETER *(Smiles.)*

Temporarily.

ANN

Ah, well. I look at you—deep asleep, not dreaming.
(Suddenly more enthusiastic.)
Did you know that when you sleep you're paralyzed? In *deep* sleep, I mean, not the dreaming, but deep sleep, your body is entirely paralyzed, except for the automatic stuff?, the breathing?, the heart? Just a fraction of one ear, so you can hear doom sneaking up, I guess—and something else, I can't remember what. You're entirely paralyzed?

PETER *(Fact.)*

Yes; I knew that.

ANN *(Surprised; disappointed.)*

You *did?!*

PETER

Yes; we published that book on sleep. Keep up.

ANN

Damn!

PETER

Sort of a sleeper.
(Nudge.)
Joke?

ANN

Damn. What? Yes: joke.

PETER

What's the other thing? The other part? I don't remember.

ANN

What?

PETER

A part of one toe?

ANN

A fraction of *some*thing.

PETER

What? *Come* on.

ANN

I don't remember. Keep up! Your *dick*, probably.

PETER

Hunh! I doubt it.

ANN

No mind of its own? No automatic . . . whatever?

PETER

I think . . .
    (Stops.)

ANN *(Engaged.)*
What! You think what!

PETER *(Pause; shakes his head.)*
No.

ANN *(Pleased; teasing.)*
Come on!

PETER

No, now.

ANN

I won't tell anyone.

PETER

Well . . . I think my circumcision is going away.
    (ANN: *long, slow facial response; giggles ending in
    guffaws.* PETER *rises, moves to leave the room.*)
All right! *All* right!

ANN *(Coming down from it.)*
No, now! Wait!
(He pauses.)
Wait. You think . . . what?
(Giggles again.)
You think your circumcision is doing *what?*
(Chuckles.)

PETER
It's not *funny!*

ANN *(Sober face.)*
No; of course not.
(Guffaws.)

PETER *(Shutting down.)*
All right! That's it!

ANN *(A hand out.)*
No, no: I'm sorry.

PETER *(A silence, then very objective.)*
I think my circumcision is . . . going away.
(Sits.)

ANN
My goodness!
(Stifles laugh.)

PETER
Please?

ANN
Sorry.

PETER
You may not have noticed.

ANN

Well, no; certainly if I had I would have noticed—that I *had.*

PETER

It's just that . . . when I . . . take it out to pee—my penis?

ANN *(Holding on.)*

Yes; I gathered.

PETER

. . . the foreskin looks to be . . . coming over the ridge of the, you know. The glans . . . just a little.

ANN *(No comment.)*

My goodness.

PETER

And when I'm sitting on the bed—when I'm naked?—I look down and it looks even more so, more of the glans seems covered.

ANN *(No comment.)*

Gracious.

PETER *(Senses derision.)*

Well, it may not mean much to *you,* but . . .

ANN

No, it does! I mean . . . goodness, if you've had a circumcised husband all these years and all of a sudden there's a foreskin waving at you, you're bound to wonder. I mean . . . who *is* this? *What* is *this?*

PETER

It's not that . . . there *is* no foreskin—as such. It's that . . . *it* seems to be . . .

ANN

It?

PETER

My penis? My penis seems to be . . . retreating.

> *(Pause.)*

A little.

> *(Pause.)*

Not much.

> *(Pause.)*

But . . . a little.

ANN *(Considers it.)*

That's so sad.

> *(Pause; helpful.)*

Time.

PETER

Hm?

ANN

Time. Things happen, as the man said.

PETER

I just thought I'd mention it.

ANN *(Cheerful.)*

Certainly! Do you . . . do you want to have it looked at?

> *(More or less suppresses a giggle.)*

Professionally, I mean?

PETER

No, I'll . . . I'll keep an eye on it.

ANN *(Can't help herself.)*

I *would;* I mean . . .

> *(Musical.)*

"The thrill of your glans . . . "

PETER

All right!

ANN *(Helpful.)*

Darling, if you want to regrow your foreskin . . .

PETER

I do *not* want to regrow my *fore*skin!

ANN

I mean, I'm sure there are ways to . . .

PETER *(Rather ugly.)*

Yeah, I know: hanging weights on it . . . for *years!* I've read about it.

ANN

Hanging weight on your . . . but it isn't even there!

PETER

What isn't?

ANN

Your foreskin. Except you say it's coming back and . . .

PETER

That's *not* what I said. What I said was that my circumcision was going away. I did not say my foreskin was coming back. For Christ's sake! It can't! It's gone! A doctor took a pair of scissors and . . .

ANN

A scalpel, I think.

PETER

Whatever! I was a baby! Nobody *asked* me! They just . . . took it *away!*

ANN

And you not even Jewish.

PETER *(Glum nod.)*

And me not even Jewish.

  (Angry.)

They should ask!

ANN

You weren't a week old, for God's sake.

PETER

I mean *wait*. They should wait . . . and ask.

ANN

How long?

PETER

You mean . . . ?

ANN

What? Until you're what—five? "Honey, do you think you'd like
to be circumcised now?" "What's *that*, Mommy?" "Well, darling,
they take a little knife and . . . "

PETER *(Not amused.)*

No; no. *Later.*

ANN

The age of reason? Sixteen, or whatever? "Hey, Pete, you think
you'd like to have your foreskin cut off today?" "Are you *kidding?!*"

PETER *(Shakes his head.)*

There'd be a lot more uncircumcised guys around.

ANN *(Fact.)*

And a lot more cervical cancer.

PETER

Really?

ANN *(Nods.)*

Some. What brought this on—me and my breasts?

PETER *(Shrugs.)*

Maybe. *I* don't know.

ANN

It's not your subject.

PETER

What?

ANN

Sex stuff.

PETER

No; I guess not.

ANN *(An assessment, but not unkind.)*

Mr. Circumspection.

PETER

Mmmmmm. Anyway—I thought I'd bring it up.

ANN

Well, I'm glad you did.

PETER

Really? Are you really glad?

ANN

What!

PETER

That I brought it up—my circumcision going away, or seeming to.

ANN *(Thinks.)*

Same thing . . . no?

PETER *(Wry smile.)*

Not your field.

ANN

Well, clearly you *wanted* to bring it up; clearly it's been bothering you.

PETER

Not bothering . . . bemusing. *Bemusing* me.

ANN

Whatever. I appreciate being told—your . . . sharing.

PETER

You're welcome. Obviously it wasn't noticed.

ANN

"Noticed"?

PETER

Never mind.

ANN

I'm sorry.

PETER

It's all right.

ANN *(After a silence.)*

Do they ask the parents? At the hospital? Before they do it?

PETER

What?

ANN

Circumcision.

PETER

I don't know. We have daughters . . . remember?

ANN

Yes. I think I remember reading it's . . . customary.

PETER

What?

ANN

Doing it.

PETER

You could *sue;* I could *sue.*

ANN *(Smiles.)*

And what would they do . . . sew it back on?

PETER

Maybe.

ANN

You mean you think they've kept it around for the past—
what?—forty-five years . . . in a bottle somewhere?

PETER

What?!

ANN

Your foreskin. In a bottle somewhere in case you sued them?

PETER

Don't be silly.

ANN

I wonder what we'd have done if we'd had a son.

PETER

What? Circumcision?

ANN

Yes. If they'd asked us.

PETER *(Short pause.)*

Damned if *I* know.

ANN *(Gruff voice; imitating.)*

"Well, sir, that's a fine bouncing baby boy you've got there!"

PETER

I've never understood "bouncing." They don't . . . bounce it, do
they? To see if . . .

ANN

Don't be silly: it's a figure of speech—*your* field.
  (*Imitation again.*)
". . . fine bouncing baby boy! Shall we trim its penis for you—
for *him?*"

PETER

I'd say "no." If they came *at* me like that, I'd say "no."

ANN

Hmmmm. I suppose I'd leave it up to you.

PETER

Male stuff, eh?

ANN

There *are* things.

PETER

And there are woman things, too? Things you and the girls talk
about and make decisions; things I don't know about?

ANN

Don't be silly: they're barely teenagers. This isn't Africa; we
don't circumcise our daughters.

PETER

That's disgusting—what they do—those tribes do!

ANN

Yes.
  (*Pause.*)
It cuts down on the infidelity, though.

PETER

What does?

ANN

Circumcising the girls—and they don't usually do it at birth.
They wait—until puberty I think.

PETER

Ugh!

ANN

Then they do it—hack off the clitoris.

PETER

Stop!

ANN

Kills all the sensation—all the pleasure, when they're old
enough for pleasure. Cuts down on infidelity, as I said. No
pleasure, no reason—no *physical* reason.

PETER

So does cutting off the breasts.

ANN

*Hack*ing.

PETER

Yes.

ANN

Circle!

PETER

Hm?

ANN

Full circle.

PETER *(Smiles.)*

Oh. Yes.
    (Pause.)
What did you want—when you came in?

ANN

When?

PETER

When you came *in*.

ANN

When?!

PETER

When you came in with the dish towel. "We should talk," you said.

ANN *(Puzzled.)*

Did I?

PETER

Yes!

ANN

Well, I must have wanted to talk about something.

PETER

Yes; I assumed.

ANN

And we didn't talk about it.

PETER

No; I don't think so.

ANN

I wonder what it was. Was this before the spinach?

PETER

During.

ANN

I wonder what it *was!*

PETER

Maybe if you go out and come back . . .

ANN

That's silly.

PETER

It might jog your memory.

ANN *(Pause.)*

All right. I'll go back out and come back in.

PETER

And I'll go back to my book.

ANN

OK.

(*She exits.* PETER *reads. She reenters.*)

We should talk.

(PETER *reads. She exits, reenters.*)

That didn't do a thing.

PETER

Nothing?

ANN

Well, it had a kind of fascination—pretending to be doing something for the first time. *That* was interesting, but I don't think it
helped much, helped our problem . . . our dilemma.

PETER

. . . the dilemma of what you meant when . . .

ANN

. . . when I came in back there and said "We should talk." The
first time. Not the second. *Before* the spinach.

PETER

I wouldn't keep doing it.

ANN

No; certainly not. Besides, it'll probably come to me, when I
least expect it, like so much does.

PETER

. . . down on the elevator, out the door, down Seventy-fourth
Street to the corner . . .

ANN

. . . stand there? Scream? In the night? Then it might come back
to me?

PETER

Might.
    (*Imitation.*)
"I know what I wanted to talk to him about!"

ANN

More likely something less . . . dramatic. But if it did—if it
was—I'd have to wake you up and tell you.

PETER

And if you *did*—if you woke me—I'd know it was something
important—something . . . threatening.

ANN (*Smiles.*)
Really; and we don't have that, *do* we.

PETER (*Uncertain.*)
No. I don't think so—not yet anyway.

ANN

No, but if I *did* wake you, said we had to talk, you'd sit up
quickly, and your eyes'd be open very wide.

PETER

Yes. Well, I *think* so. And I'd know something terrible had
happened.

ANN

You'd *know?*

PETER

Well, no; I don't know if I'd *know,* but I *think* I would.

ANN

You'd assume.

PETER

Yes. That's it: I'd assume.

ANN

What would you assume?

PETER

That something terrible had . . .

ANN

You *said* that. Spe*cifi*cally. What specifically?

PETER *(A little annoyed.)*
Well, I don't know. I mean . . . for God's sake, Ann . . .

ANN

I'm not a generality; I'm a *person.*

PETER

I *know.*

ANN

. . . and if I woke you and you bolted up, whatever awful thing
you thought had happened would relate to *me,* most likely, or
the kids, or you, or . . .

PETER

Yes!

ANN

So?!

PETER

I'd . . . what's the term? . . . I'd "gather my wits about me."

ANN

So that's what you'd do, is it?

PETER

What?

ANN

Gather your wits about you—if I sat on the bed and woke you in the . . . what do they call it? . . . the small hours? That's what you'd do?

PETER

Most likely. Or scream. Or refuse to wake up.

ANN

If you thought it was going to be terrible enough.

PETER

Yes. But I'd probably bolt up, gather my wits about me . . . and ask what it was.

ANN

But what would you *imagine*? What would you imagine was terrible enough . . .

PETER

That's not what I said. "Important" is what I said, or "threatening."

ANN

Then you said "terrible."

PETER

All *right!!*

ANN

And we don't *have* that, *do* we?

PETER *(Sighs.)*

No. But—as I said—we're probably going to, one day.

ANN *(Sincere.)*

Oh, you poor dear. And we may even talk about it.

PETER

Don't patronize.

ANN

I'm *not*.

PETER *(Calm.)*

I'm not a bad person, you know; my life may not be very exciting . . . no jagged edges . . .

ANN *(Agreeing.)*

No.

PETER

. . . but it's not a bad life we've made together, and . . .

ANN

I *know!* I'm *happy!*

PETER *(Tiny pause.)*

Are you?

ANN

Well . . . yes; I . . . yes, of course. I have my bad times. You do, too.

PETER

You *do?*

ANN

Of course. You never tell me about *yours*, so . . .

PETER

I *do!* I just told you about . . .

ANN

Not the real ones; not the ones that there's nothing to be done about . . . in any real sense.

PETER *(Pause.)*

Ah. Those. Well, you don't tell me, *either.*

ANN

About the real ones? The ones there's nothing to be done
about?

PETER

Yes; those.

ANN

Why bother? If there's nothing to be done . . . why bother? If
there's no help . . . why bother?

PETER *(Shy.)*

To . . . share?

ANN

Be helpless together? Cling like marmosets?

PETER

People need that sometimes.

ANN

Do they? *Do* you?

PETER

Not yet . . . I guess.

ANN

I wonder if *I* do.

PETER *(Pressing.)*

What was it you'd *tell* me?

ANN *(Self-absorbed.)*

Hm?

PETER

What was it you'd tell me if you sat on the bed and woke me in
the small hours? What might it *be?*

ANN

Oh . . .

(Gathers ideas.)

that my mother had died—or yours? That someone had kidnapped the girls? That I was three months pregnant and not by you? That our broker had made off with everything? That . . .

PETER *(Hands over ears.)*

Please!!

ANN

What do you want—minor stuff? The parakeets got out? The icebox broke? Someone threw up in the hall?

PETER

Yes!

ANN

I wouldn't wake you up for any of that. And I don't wake you for the worse stuff—the real killers that nothing can be done about. That . . . that I know you love me—as you understand it, and I'm grateful for that—but not *enough,* that you don't love me the way I need it, or I think I do; that that's not your makeup—not *in* you, perhaps, or that maybe there's no one could do it, could love me as much as I *need* to be loved; or *worse* . . . that I think I deserve more than I do, and that deep down I'm . . . *less* than I think I am.

PETER *(A hand out.)*

Oh, Ann.

ANN

Shall I go on?

PETER *(Sighs.)*

Might as well.

ANN

That nothing is . . . ultimately . . . sufficient—not you, not us, not . . . me? And I know you're probably going through this, too. Or—worse—that maybe you're *not,* that maybe none of it's ever occurred to you—that you . . . don't have it *in* you?

PETER *(Long silence.)*

Well.

ANN

You did *ask*.

PETER

Yes, I did.

ANN

Which is it?

PETER

Pardon?

ANN *(Harder.)*

. . . that you don't have it in you!

PETER *(Quiet supplication.)*

Be kind.

ANN

No! No! *Do* you? Do you have it in you?

PETER *(Engaged, but rational.)*

I thought we both made a decision—when we decided to be together, or even before we knew each other—I thought we made a decision, *must* have made one, that what we wanted was a smooth voyage on a safe ship, a view of porpoises now and then, a gentle swell, bright clouds way off, a sense that it was a . . . familiar voyage, though we'd never taken it before—a pleasant journey, all the way through. And that's what we're having . . .

(*Slight doubt.*)

isn't it?

ANN *(A tinge of disappointment.)*

Yeah; sure.

PETER *(Hearing it.)*

No?

ANN

No; *yes.* That's what we've both wanted: stay away from ice-
bergs; avoid the Bermuda Triangle; remember where the
lifeboats are, knowing, of course, that most of them don't
work—no need. Yes; that's what we've wanted . . . and that's
what we've had—for the most part. And isn't it frightening.

PETER

That wasn't a question.

ANN

No; it wasn't. And isn't it frightening.

PETER *(A little boy.)*

It is?

ANN

Sure. And we'll never die.

PETER

No?

ANN

No; we'll just vanish.
　　(A silence.)

PETER

I made the assumption, I guess, that it's what you wanted, too.

ANN

Oh? Well . . . sure—for the most part . . . *most* of the time. We
have a better life than most people; we haven't hit any of the brick
walls yet; the playing field is all green and mowed within an inch
of its life, except now and then there are . . . gopher holes.

PETER *(Bewildered.)*

Gopher holes?!

ANN

Sure; take our fucking, now . . .

PETER *(A protest.)*

Ann!

ANN

There's no one here: The cats are asleep someplace, the girls are upstairs going deaf from all the music, and the birds couldn't care less. Who's to hear?

PETER *(Quietly.)*

Me?

ANN

Oh, yeah? Then listen. You're good at making love.

PETER

Thank you.

ANN

You're welcome, but you're lousy at fucking.

(PETER *gets up.*)

Sit down!

(He does.)

All the things that fucking entails, or *can* entail—aggressive, brutal maybe, two people who've known each other for years— slept together for years—suddenly behaving like strangers, like people who've just met in a bar and gone to the motel next door to hammer it all out, to fuck for the sake of fucking. There are people who've lived together for years, who love one another deeply. Who sometimes go at each other like strangers—a regular one-shot deal, like you'll never see each other again . . . or *want* to. The moment! Two strangers! The moment! There are people rise to that—sink to it, if you like—*rise* to that, become animals, *strangers*, with nothing less than impure simple lust for one another. There are people *do* that.

PETER *(Long, sad pause.)*

I'm not like that.

ANN

I know. And I love you dearly. When we come together in bed
and I know we're going to—what is the term young people
use?—going to *do* it? When we come together in bed and I
know we're going to "make love." I know it's going to be two
people who love each other giving quiet, orderly, predictable,
deeply pleasurable joy. And believe me, my darling, it's enough;
it's *more* than enough . . . most of the time. But where's the . . .
the rage, the . . . animal? We're animals! Why don't we behave
like that . . . like beasts?! Is it that we love each other too safely, maybe? That we're secure? That we're too . . . civilized? Don't
we ever *hate* one another?

PETER *(Small pause.)*

Cover it up any way you want—be nice about it—but you mean
I'm not very good in bed.

ANN

No! You're very *good*—*very* good. I just wish you could be a lit-
tle . . . *bad* sometime.
　　(Sees him react.)
I've *hurt* you!

PETER

No; that's not it. I *was* bad, once. I was *very* bad.

ANN *(Ears sharp.)*

Oh? Recently?

PETER *(Smiles slightly.)*

No; before I knew you.

ANN *(Kind of sad.)*

Oh.

PETER

I've never told you. I never thought I'd have to. I was at college.
And I'd pledged to a fraternity.

ANN *(Generous.)*

Well . . . back then bright people *did* that sometimes.

PETER

Yes. And there was a lot of hazing—forcing beer down us 'til we threw up, making us take terrible enemas until we couldn't hold it, and throwing us out of doors naked, so passersby would . . .

ANN

Jesus!

PETER

Yes; well. And one night there was the sex party.

ANN *(Ears again.)*

Oh?

PETER

It was ugly; it was planned with one of the sororities. The pledges were all put together—the girls *with* the boys, and . . .

ANN

And?

PETER

And we were supposed to fuck. Cherry-popping they called it.

ANN

I don't believe it.

PETER

What happened?

ANN

No; the term.

PETER

Well, there it was—a lot of liquor, grass, other stuff. Mattresses spread around; lights way down; rooms, too. And most people . . . *wanted* it, or seemed to.

ANN

What fraternity *was* this?

PETER

And there was this girl came on to me; I didn't know her . . .

ANN

. . . from Eve.

PETER

. . . from what? Oh; yes; very good. I didn't know her and she'd
brought me into this room, and we were alone in there and . . .
well, I'd *been* with a couple of girls—you know: in my life—so I
wasn't a *total* amateur, or anything. And we were both . . . *out* of
it—mostly grass, I think—and we'd gotten naked, and she was
playing with my . . . with my . . .

ANN

Your ear? Your toe?

PETER

No; my . . . my . . .
    (*Points.*)

ANN (*Fairly loud.*)

Your penis!

PETER (*Sotto voce.*)

Yes! Shhhhh!
    (*She laughs.*)
Don't!

ANN

Sorry.

PETER

And I guess we were both pretty hot, and I moved down on her
and . . .

ANN

Did she like that? *I* do.

PETER

I know.

ANN

Go on.

PETER

Well, I thought she *would,* and I was spreading her a little, and she said, "No. Don't do that. Go *in* me." And so I spread her further, and, and, well, my . . . penis was very hard, and I was going to enter her and she said, "No; not there. The *other.*"

ANN *(Enlightened.)*

Ohhhhhh.

PETER

"You want me to . . . ," "Yes! Yes! There!" Well, I'd never done that, and . . .

ANN

What a surprise.

PETER

Let me finish?

ANN

Sorry.

PETER

But it was what she wanted she said, and it was real exciting, and so I did. And it *was;* it was real exciting, and disgusting, and it turned me on in an awful way, and I wanted to hurt her, and she started sort of hissing at me, "Hurt me! Hurt me!" And . . . I guess I was too big . . .

ANN *(Entranced.)*

Big enough.

PETER

And—here it is—I was stroking harder and harder, jamming it into her, really, and she was sobbing and yelling and "Yes! Hurt me!" And I kept on jamming and jamming into her until she screamed, and it wasn't a right scream, and she screamed again and tried to push me out with her hands and she did, and there was blood; my . . . penis was bloody and . . .

ANN *(Oddly angry.)*

No! Not your *penis!* Your dick! Your cock! *That's* what was bloody!

PETER *(Tiny pause.)*

Yes;

(Comes down from it as he talks.)

and I was all bloody, and she was crying—whimpering really, and I said, "Oh, God, I'm sorry; I'm so sorry!" And she said, "You hurt me!" And I said "That's what you said; you said you wanted me to hurt you! I'm sorry! I'm so sorry!"

(Pause.)

ANN *(Cold.)*

What happened?

PETER *(Sighs.)*

She went to the infirmary, they told me, and they fixed her up and . . .

ANN

And?

PETER

And she never told anyone who I was. I guess she was too embarrassed.

ANN

Or too nice?

PETER

What? Oh, yes: or too nice. So . . . so I've been careful never to hurt anyone—to hurt *you;* you being everyone for so long now.

ANN

Thank you.

PETER
It's not all right to want to love somebody and not hurt them?

ANN *(Oddly self-absorbed.)*
Yes; of course it is.

PETER
So, if I've been too careful, if I'm too gentle . . .

ANN
You learned your lesson.

PETER
Yes.

ANN
I don't think I was talking about pain, anyway—not like *that;* that's something I don't need. I think I was talking about being an animal—nothing more.

PETER *(A litle uncertain.)*
We all are, no?

ANN
Yes, but we can have it bred out of us—learned away. Thank you for being a fine husband—no sarcasm; don't even *think* it—for being gentle, and thoughtful, and honest, and . . . "good"—oh, that awful word! And for putting up with your wife, who seems to want . . . something a little less—less deserving, maybe, though she doesn't know; has glimmers now and then, but doesn't truly know.

PETER *(Pause.)*
You're welcome.

ANN *(Objective now.)*
All these years and you never told me.

PETER *(A slight smile.)*
Ditto.

ANN *(Smiles; nods.)*
Touché.

PETER

There are things you don't say if they don't have anything to do
with anything that's ever going to happen again.

ANN

They're not cautionary, you mean.

PETER

Yes . . . no.

ANN *(Smiles.)*

Yes . . . no.

(Pause.)

I *am* happy with you—with us. It's me I sense I'm not happy
with—not entirely. And I never know exactly what it is; something . . . *other.*

PETER *(Gentle.)*

And no one can help?

ANN

No. No one . . . this "something other."

PETER

Almost anything?

ANN *(Tiny, sharp laugh.)*

You mean almost *anyone?* No; not at all. Something less,
maybe. Maybe it's just being secure; maybe *that's* the killer. It's
not pain I want, or loss; it's what I can't imagine—but I imagine
imagining.

PETER *(Smile.)*

It's hopeless, then.

ANN

Yes. Isn't that nice? If it can't be helped why fret it?

PETER *(Pause.)*

Has this helped? All of this . . . has it helped?

ANN *(Rising.)*

Yes; a little.

*(Goes to him, looks at him in the face, smiles, slaps
him hard. His mouth opens in astonishment; she
kisses his cheek where she slapped him.)*

Did that hurt?

PETER *(Feels his cheek.)*

Yes.

ANN *(Bemused.)*

I've never done that, *have* I.

PETER *(Why?)*

No!

ANN

No; I've never wanted to, and I didn't *want* to *now*—*hurt* you,
I mean. Astonish you, I think. Yes: astonish you. Did that astonish you?

PETER

In that I've never imagined it? Yes.

ANN

Then that must be what I wanted—a little . . . disorder around
here, a little . . . chaos.

PETER

And we don't have that.

ANN

No. A little madness. Wouldn't that be good?

PETER *(Rising to it.)*

How would we go about it?

ANN

About what?

PETER

The chaos! The madness!

ANN

How would we go *about* it?

PETER *(Growing enthusiasm.)*
Yes! What would happen!

ANN *(As if recalling.)*
You'd be reading; I'd come in, and the lights would start blink-ing, and the chandeliers would start swaying . . .

PETER

An *earth*quake!

ANN

No . . . a tor*nado!* And we'd hear it coming—the roaring we'd never heard before but knew what it was!

PETER

And I'd go to the window, and there it was! Coming right at us!

ANN

And it would be terrifying and exciting, and it would sweep us all away, shatter the windows, rip the pictures from the walls...!

PETER *(Fully caught up.)*
. . . knock over the cages and the birds would fly out . . .

ANN

. . . and the cats would see that, and they would catch the para-keets and *eat* them! . . .

PETER

. . . and the girls would see this, and the girls would do—what?!—eat the cats?

ANN

Sure; fearful symmetry.

PETER

And what . . . and what do *we* do then . . . eat the girls?

ANN *(Gleefully abandoned.)*

Sure! Even more fearful!

(Down now, both of them; laughter subsiding, fading into a silence.)

PETER *(Finally.)*

But who will eat us?

ANN *(Pause.)*

We do that ourselves. We eat ourselves—all up.

PETER *(Long pause.)*

Gobble gobble.

ANN *(Sad smile.)*

Gobble.

(PETER laughs—harshly; abruptly; stops. Long pause; she rises, moves toward the kitchen. Don't rush any of the remaining.)

I think I'll try doing the spinach again.

(Pause.)

Or maybe I won't.

(Pause.)

What are you going to do? Read?

PETER

I don't know. It's a nice day; maybe I'll go to the park—read there. Something readable.

ANN

Don't be forever.

PETER

(Rises, moves toward the front door with the book.)

No; no, I won't.

ANN *(Pause.)*

I love you, you know.

PETER *(Pause.)*

Yes; I know. And I love you.

ANN *(Exiting.)*

Don't take any wooden nickels.

PETER

(Registering, after she exits.)

Don't take any what? Ann?

(But she is gone. He pauses, exits to hall to front door.)

END OF ACT ONE

ACT TWO

THE ZOO STORY

*Central Park. There are two benches. As the curtain
rises,* PETER *is seated on the downstage bench. He is
reading a book. He stops reading, cleans his glasses,
goes back to reading.* JERRY *enters.*

JERRY

I've been to the zoo.
> (PETER *doesn't notice.*)

I said, I've been to the zoo. MISTER! I'VE BEEN TO THE
ZOO!

PETER

Hm? . . . What? . . . I'm sorry, were you talking to me?

JERRY

I went to the zoo, and then I walked until I came here. Have I
been walking north?

PETER *(Puzzled.)*

North? Why . . . I . . . I think so. Let me see.

JERRY *(Pointing past the audience.)*

Is that Fifth Avenue?

PETER

Why yes; yes, it is.

JERRY

And what is that cross street there; that one, to the right?

PETER

That? Oh, that's Seventy-fourth Street.

JERRY

And the zoo is around Sixty-fifth Street; so, I've been walking north.

PETER

(*Anxious to get back to his reading.*)
Yes; it would seem so.

JERRY

Good old north.

PETER *(Lightly, by reflex.)*

Ha, ha.

JERRY *(After a slight pause.)*
But not due north.

PETER

I . . . well, no, not due north; but, we . . . call it north. It's northerly.

JERRY

(*Watches as* PETER, *anxious to dismiss him, prepares his pipe.*)
Well, boy; *you're* not going to get lung cancer, are you?

PETER

(*Looks up, a little annoyed, then smiles.*)
No, sir. Not from this.

JERRY

No, sir. What you'll probably get is cancer of the mouth, and then you'll have to wear one of those things Freud wore after they took one whole side of his jaw away. What do they call those things?

PETER *(Uncomfortable.)*

A prosthesis?

JERRY

The very thing! A prosthesis. You're an educated man, aren't you? Are you a doctor?

PETER

Oh, no; no. I read about it somewhere; *Time* magazine, I think.
(He turns to his book.)

JERRY

Well, *Time* magazine isn't for blockheads.

PETER

No, I suppose not.

JERRY *(After a pause.)*
Boy, I'm glad that's Fifth Avenue there.

PETER *(Vaguely.)*
Yes.

JERRY

I don't like the west side of the park much.

PETER

Oh?
(Then, slightly wary, but interested.)
Why?

JERRY *(Offhand.)*
I don't know.

PETER

Oh.
(He returns to his book.)

JERRY

(He stands for a few seconds, looking at PETER, *who finally looks up again, puzzled.)*
Do you mind if we talk?

PETER *(Obviously minding.)*

Why . . . no, no.

JERRY

Yes, you do; you do.

PETER

(Puts his book down, his pipe away, and smiling.)
No, really; I don't mind.

JERRY

Yes you do.

PETER *(Finally decided.)*
No; I don't mind at all, really.

JERRY

It's . . . it's a nice day.

PETER *(Stares unnecessarily at the sky.)*
Yes. Yes, it is; lovely.

JERRY

I've been to the zoo.

PETER

Yes, I think you said so . . . didn't you?

JERRY

I bet you've got TV, huh?

PETER

Why, yes, we have two; one for the children.

JERRY

You're married!

PETER *(With pleased emphasis.)*
Why, certainly.

JERRY

It isn't a law, for God's sake.

PETER

No . . . no, of course not.

JERRY

And you have a wife.

PETER

(Bewildered by the seeming lack of communication.)
Yes!

JERRY

And you have children.

PETER

Yes; two.

JERRY

Boys?

PETER

No, girls . . . both girls.

JERRY

But you wanted boys.

PETER

Well . . . naturally, every man wants a son, but . . .

JERRY *(Lightly mocking.)*
But that's the way the cookie crumbles?

PETER *(Annoyed.)*
I wasn't going to say that.

JERRY

And you're not going to have any more kids, are you?

PETER *(A bit distantly.)*

No. No more.

    (Then back, and irksome.)

Why did you say that? How would you know about that?

JERRY

The way you cross your legs, perhaps; something in the voice. Or maybe I'm just guessing. Is it your wife?

PETER *(Furious.)*

That's none of your business!

    (A silence.)

Do you understand?

    (JERRY nods. PETER is quiet now.)

Well, you're right. We'll have no more children.

JERRY *(Softly.)*

That *is* the way the cookie crumbles.

PETER *(Forgiving.)*

Yes . . . I guess so.

JERRY

Do you mind if I ask you questions?

PETER

Oh, not really.

JERRY

I'll tell you why I do it; I don't talk to many people—except to say like: Give me a beer, or where's the john, or what time does the feature go on, or keep your hands to yourself, buddy. You know—things like that.

PETER

I must say I don't . . .

JERRY

But every once in awhile I like to talk to somebody, really *talk;* like to get to know somebody, know all about him.

PETER

(Lightly laughing, still a little uncomfortable.)
And am I the guinea pig for today?

JERRY

On a sun-drenched Sunday afternoon like this? Who better than a nice married man with two daughters and . . . uh . . . a dog?
    (PETER shakes his head.)
No? Two dogs.
    (PETER shakes his head again.)
Hm. No dogs?
    (PETER shakes his head, sadly.)
Oh, that's a shame. But you look like an animal man. CATS?
    (PETER nods his head, ruefully.)
Cats! But, that can't be your idea. No, sir. Your wife and daughters?
    (PETER nods his head.)
Is there anything else I should know?

PETER *(He has to clear his throat.)*
There are . . . there are two parakeets. One . . . uh . . . one for each of my daughters.

JERRY

Birds.

PETER

My daughters keep them in a cage in their bedroom.

JERRY

Do they carry disease? The birds.

PETER

I don't believe so.

JERRY

That's too bad. If they did you could set them loose in the house and the cats could eat them and die, maybe.

(PETER *looks blank for a moment, then laughs.*)

And what else? What do you do to support your enormous household?

PETER

I . . . uh . . . I have an executive position with a . . . a small publishing house. We . . . uh . . . publish textbooks.

JERRY

That sounds nice; very nice. What do you make?

PETER *(Still cheerful.)*

Now look here!

JERRY

Oh, come on.

PETER

Well, I make around two hundred thousand a year, but I don't carry more than forty dollars at any one time . . . in case you're a . . . a holdup man . . . ha, ha, ha.

JERRY *(Ignoring the above.)*

Where do you live?

(PETER *is reluctant.*)

Oh, look; I'm not going to rob you, and I'm not going to kidnap your parakeets, your cats, or your daughters.

PETER *(Too loud.)*

I live between Lexington and Third Avenue, on Seventy-fourth Street.

JERRY

That wasn't so hard, was it?

PETER

I didn't mean to seem . . . ah . . . it's that you don't really carry
on a conversation; you just ask questions. And I'm . . . I'm nor-
mally . . . uh . . . reticent. Why do you just stand there?

JERRY

I'll start walking around in a little while, and maybe later I'll sit
down. Say, what's the dividing line between upper-middle-mid-
dle-class and lower-upper-middle-class?

PETER

My dear fellow, I . . .

JERRY

Don't my dear fellow me.

PETER *(Unhappily.)*

Was I patronizing? I believe I was; I'm sorry. But, you see, your
question about the classes bewildered me.

JERRY

And when you're bewildered you become patronizing?

PETER

I . . . I don't express myself too well, sometimes.
      (He attempts a joke on himself.)
I'm in publishing, not writing.

JERRY *(Amused, but not at the humor.)*

So be it. The truth *is:* I was being patronizing.

PETER

Oh, now; you needn't say that.
      (It is at this point that JERRY *may begin to move about
      the stage with slowly increasing determination and
      authority, but pacing himself, so that the long speech
      about the dog comes at the high point of the arc.)*

JERRY

All right. Who are your favorite writers? Baudelaire and Stephen King?

PETER *(Wary.)*

Well, I like a great many writers; I have a considerable . . . catholicity of taste, if I may say so. Those two men are fine, each in his way.

　　(Warming up.)

Baudelaire, of course . . . uh . . . is by far the finer of the two, but Stephen King has a place . . . in our . . . uh . . . national . . . .

JERRY

Skip it.

PETER

I . . . sorry.

JERRY

Do you know what I did before I went to the zoo today? I walked all the way up Fifth Avenue from Washington Square; all the way.

PETER

Oh; you live in Greenwich Village!

　　(This seems to enlighten PETER.*)*

JERRY

No, I don't. I took the subway down to the Village so I could walk all the way up Fifth Avenue to the zoo. It's one of those things a person has to do; sometimes a person has to go a very long distance out of his way to come back a short distance correctly.

PETER *(Almost pouting.)*

Oh, I thought you lived in Greenwich Village.

JERRY

What were you trying to do? Make sense out of things? Bring order? The old pigeonhole bit? Well, that's easy; I'll tell you. I live in a four-story brownstone rooming-house on the upper West Side between Columbus Avenue and Central Park West. I live on the top floor; rear; west. It's a laughably small room, and one of my walls is made of beaverboard; this beaverboard separates my room from another laughably small room, so I assume that the two rooms were once one room, a small room, but not necessarily laughable. The room beyond my beaverboard wall is occupied by a black queen who always keeps his door open; well, not always, but *always* when he's plucking his eyebrows, which he does with Buddhist concentration. This black queen has rotten teeth, which is rare, and he has a Japanese kimono, which is also pretty rare; and he wears his kimono to and from the john in the hall, which is pretty frequent. I mean, he goes to the john a lot. He never bothers me, and he never brings anyone up to his room. All he does is pluck his eyebrows, wear his kimono and go to the john. Now, the two front rooms on my floor are a little larger, I guess; but they're pretty small, too. There's a Puerto Rican family in one of them, a husband, a wife, and some kids; I don't know how many. These people entertain a lot. And in the other front room, there's somebody living there, but I don't know who it is. I've never seen who it is. Never. Never ever.

PETER *(Embarrassed.)*

Why . . . why do you live there?

JERRY *(From a distance.)*

I don't know.

PETER

It doesn't sound like a very nice place . . . where you live.

JERRY

Well, no; it isn't an apartment in the East Seventies. But, then again, I don't have one wife, two daughters, two cats and two parakeets. What I do have, I have toilet articles, a few clothes, a hot plate that I'm not supposed to have, a can opener, one that works with a key, you know; a knife, two forks, and two spoons, one small, one large; three plates, a cup, a saucer, a drinking glass, two picture frames, both empty, eight or nine books, a pack of pornographic playing cards, regular deck, an old Western Union typewriter that prints nothing but capital letters, and a small strongbox without a lock which has in it . . . what? Rocks! Some rocks . . . sea-rounded rocks I picked up on the beach when I was a kid. Under which . . . weighed down . . . are some letters . . . please letters . . . please why don't you do this, and please why don't you do that letters. And when letters, too. When will you write? When will you come? When? These letters are from more recent years.

PETER *(Stares glumly at his shoes, then:)*
About those two empty picture frames . . . ?

JERRY
I don't see why they need any explanation at all. Isn't it clear? I don't have pictures of anyone to put in them.

PETER
Your parents . . . perhaps . . . a girlfriend . . .

JERRY
You're a very sweet man, and you're possessed of a truly enviable innocence. But good old Mom and good old Pop are dead . . . you know? . . . I'm broken up about it, too . . . I mean really. BUT. That particular vaudeville act is playing the cloud circuit now, so I don't see how I can look at them, all neat and framed. Besides, or, rather, to be pointed about it, good old Mom walked out on good old Pop when I was ten and a half years old; she embarked on an adulterous turn of our southern states . . . a journey of a year's duration . . . and her most constant companion . . . among others, among many others . . . was a Mr. Barleycorn. At least, that's what good old Pop told me after he went down . . . came back . . . brought her body north. We'd received the news between Christmas and New Year's, you see, that good old Mom had parted with the ghost in some dump in Alabama. And, without the ghost . . . she was less welcome. I mean, what was she? A

stiff . . . a northern stiff. At any rate, good old Pop celebrated the
New Year for an even two weeks and then slapped into the front
of a somewhat moving city omnibus, which sort of cleaned things
out family-wise. Well no; then there was Mom's sister, who was
given neither to sin nor the consolations of the bottle. I moved in
on her, and my memory of her is slight excepting I remember still
that she did all things dourly: sleeping, eating, working, praying.
She dropped dead on the stairs to her apartment, my apartment
then, too, on the afternoon of my high school graduation. A terri-
bly middle-European joke, if you ask me.

PETER

Oh, my; oh, my.

JERRY

Oh, your what? But that was a long time ago, and I have no feeling about any of it that I care to admit to myself. Perhaps you
can see, though, why good old Mom and good old Pop are
frameless. What's your name? Your first name?

PETER

I'm Peter.

JERRY

I'd forgotten to ask you. I'm Jerry.

PETER (*With a slight nervous laugh.*)

Hello, Jerry.

JERRY (*Nods his hello.*)

And let's see now; what's the point of having a girl's picture,
especially in two frames? I have two picture frames, you
remember. I never see the pretty little ladies more than once,
and most of them wouldn't be caught in the same room with a
camera. It's odd, and I wonder if it's sad.

PETER

The girls?

JERRY

No. I wonder if it's sad that I never see the little ladies more
than once. I've never been able to have sex with, or, how is it
put? . . . make love to anybody more than once. Once; that's it
. . . Oh, wait; for a week and a half, when I was fifteen . . .
and I hang my head in shame that puberty was late . . . I was a
h-o-m-o-s-e-x-u-a-l. I mean, I was queer . . .

(*Very fast.*)

. . . queer, queer, queer . . . with bells ringing, banners snapping
in the wind. And for those eleven days, I met at least twice a day
with the park superintendent's son . . . a Greek boy, whose birth-
day was the same as mine, except he was a year older. I think I
was very much in love . . . maybe just with sex. But that was the
jazz of a very special hotel, wasn't it? And now; oh, do I love the
little ladies; really, I love them. For about an hour.

PETER

Well, it seems perfectly simple to me, you just haven't met . . .

JERRY (*Angry.*)

Look! Are you going to tell me to get married and have parakeets?

PETER (*Angry, himself.*)

Forget the parakeets! And stay single if you want to. It's no business of mine. I didn't start this conversation in the . . .

JERRY

All right, all right. I'm sorry. All right? You're not angry?

PETER (*Laughing.*)

No, I'm not angry.

JERRY

Good. Interesting that you asked me about the picture frames.
I would have thought that you would have asked me about the
pornographic playing cards.

PETER *(With a knowing smile.)*

Oh, I've seen those cards.

JERRY

That's not the point.

   (Laughs.)

I suppose when you were a kid you and your pals passed them around, or you had a pack of your own.

PETER

Well, I guess a lot of us did.

JERRY

And you threw them away just before you got married.

PETER

Oh, now; look here. I didn't *need* anything like that when I got older.

JERRY

No?

PETER *(Embarrassed.)*

I'd rather not talk about these things.

JERRY

So? Don't. Besides, I wasn't trying to plumb your postadolescent sexual life and hard times; what I wanted to get at is the value difference between pornographic playing cards when you're a kid, and pornographic playing cards when you're older. It's that when you're a kid you use the cards as a substitute for real experience, and when you're older you use real experience as a substitute for the fantasy. But I imagine you'd rather hear about what happened at the zoo.

PETER *(Enthusiastic.)*

Oh, yes; the zoo.

   (Then awkward.)

That is . . . if you . . .

JERRY

Let me tell you about why I went . . . well, let me tell you some things. I've told you about the fourth floor of the rooming-house where I live. I think the rooms are better as you go down; floor by floor. I guess they are; I don't know. I don't know any of the people on the third and second floors. Oh, wait! I do know that there's a lady living on the third floor, in the front. I know because she cries all the time. Whenever I go out or come back in, whenever I pass her door, I always hear her crying, muffled, but . . . very determined. Very determined indeed. But the one I'm getting to, and all about the dog, is the landlady. I don't like to use words that are too harsh in describing people. I don't like to. But the landlady is a fat, ugly, mean, stupid, unwashed, misanthropic, cheap, drunken bag of garbage. And you may have noticed that I very seldom use profanity, so I can't describe her as well as I might.

PETER

You describe her . . . vividly.

JERRY

Well, thanks. Anyway, she has a dog, and she and her dog are the gatekeepers of my dwelling. The woman is bad enough; she leans around in the entrance hall, spying to see that I don't bring in things or people, and when she's had her mid-afternoon pint of lemon-flavored gin she always stops me in the hall, and grabs ahold of my coat or my arm, and she presses her disgusting body up against me to keep me in a corner so she can talk to me. The smell of her body and her breath . . . you can't imagine it . . . and somewhere, somewhere in the back of that pea-sized brain of hers, an organ developed just enough to let her eat, drink, and emit, she has some foul parody of sexual desire. And I, Peter, am the object of her sweaty lust.

PETER

That's disgusting. That's . . . horrible.

JERRY

But I have found a way to keep her off. When she talks to me, when she presses herself to my body and mumbles about her room and how I should come there, I merely say: but, Love; wasn't yesterday enough for you, and the day before? Then she puzzles, she makes slits of her tiny eyes, she sways a little, and then, Peter . . . and it is at this moment that I think I might be doing some good in that tormented house . . . a simple-minded smile begins to form on her unthinkable face, and she giggles and groans as she thinks about yesterday and the day before; as she believes and relives what never happened. Then, she motions to that black monster of a dog she has, and she goes back to her room. And I am safe until our next meeting.

PETER

It's so . . . I find it hard to believe that people such as that really *are*.

JERRY *(Lightly mocking.)*

It's for reading about, isn't it?

PETER *(Seriously.)*

Yes.

JERRY

And fact is better left to fiction. You're right, Peter. Well, what I have been meaning to tell you about is the dog; I shall, now.

PETER *(Nervously.)*

Oh yes; the dog.

JERRY

Don't go. You're not thinking of going, are you?

PETER *(Nervously.)*

Well . . . no, I don't think so.

JERRY *(As if to a child.)*

Because after I tell you about the dog, do you know what then? Then . . . then I'll tell you about what happened at the zoo.

PETER *(Laughing faintly.)*
You're . . . you're full of stories, aren't you?

JERRY
You don't *have* to listen. Nobody is holding you here; remember that. Keep that in your mind.

PETER *(Irritably.)*
I know that.

JERRY
You do? Good.

(The following speech, it seems to me, should be done with a great deal of action, to achieve a hypnotic effect on PETER, *and on the audience, too. Some specific actions have been suggested, but the director and the actor playing* JERRY *might best work it out for themselves.)*

ALL RIGHT.

(As if reading from a huge billboard.)

THE STORY OF JERRY AND THE DOG!

(Natural again.)

What I am going to tell you has something to do with how sometimes it's necessary to go a long distance out of the way in order to come back a short distance correctly; or, maybe I only think it has something do with that. But, it's why I went to the zoo today, and why I walked north . . . northerly, rather . . . until I came here. All right. The dog, I think I told you, is a black monster of a beast: an oversized head, tiny, tiny ears, and eyes . . . bloodshot, infected, maybe; and a body you can see the ribs through the skin. The dog is black, all black; all black except for the bloodshot eyes, and . . . yes . . . and an open sore on its . . . *right* forepaw; that is red, too. And, oh yes; the poor monster, and I do believe it's an old dog . . . it's certainly a misused one . . . almost always has an erection . . . of sorts. That's red, too. And . . . what else? . . . oh, yes; there's a gray-yellow-white color, too, when he bares his fangs. Like this: Grrrrrrr! Which is what he did when he saw me for the first time . . . the day I moved in. I worried about that animal the very first minute I met him. Now, animals don't take to me like Saint Francis had birds hanging off him all the time. What I mean is: Animals are indifferent to me . . . like people

(*He smiles lightly.*)

. . . most of the time. But this dog wasn't indifferent. From the very beginning he'd snarl and then go for me, to get one of my legs. Not like he was rabid, you know; he was sort of a stumbly dog, but he wasn't half-assed, either. It was a good, stumbly run; but I always got away. He got a piece of my trouser leg, look, you see right here, where it's mended; he got that the second day I lived there; but, I kicked free and got upstairs fast, so that was that.

(*Puzzles.*)

I still don't know to this day how the other roomers manage it, but you know what I *think:* I think it had only to do with me. Cozy. So. Anyway, this went on for over a week, whenever I came in; but never when I went out. That's funny. Or, it *was* funny. I could pack up and live in the street for all the dog cared. Well, I thought about it up in my room one day, one of the times after I'd bolted upstairs, and I made up my mind. I decided: First, I'll kill the dog with kindness, and if that doesn't work . . . I'll just kill him.

(PETER *winces.*)

Don't react, Peter; just listen. So, the next day I went out and bought a bag of hamburgers, medium rare, no catsup, no onion; and on the way home I threw away all the rolls and kept just the meat.

(*Action for the following, perhaps.*)

When I got back to the rooming-house the dog was waiting for me. I half opened the door that led into the entrance hall, and there it was; waiting for me. It figured. I went in, very cautiously, and I had the hamburgers, you remember; I opened the bag, and I set the meat down about twelve feet from where the dog was snarling at me. Like so! He snarled; stopped snarling; sniffed; moved slowly; then faster; then faster toward the meat. Well, when he got to it he stopped, and he looked at me. I smiled; but tentatively, you understand. He turned his face back to the hamburgers, smelled, sniffed some more, and then . . . RRRAAAAGGGGGHHHH, like that . . . he tore into them. It was as if he had never eaten anything in his life before, except like garbage. Which might very well have been the truth. I don't think the landlady ever eats anything but garbage. But. He ate all the hamburgers, almost all at once, making sounds in his throat like a woman. *Then,* when he'd finished the meat, the hamburger, and tried to eat the paper, too, he sat down and smiled. I think he smiled; I know cats do. It was a very gratifying few moments. Then, BAM, he snarled and made for me again. He didn't get me this time, either. So, I got upstairs, and I lay down on my bed and started to think about the dog again. To be truthful, I was offended, and I was damn mad, too. It was six perfectly good hamburgers with not enough pork in them to make it disgusting. I was offended. But, after a while, I decided to try it again for a few more days. If you think about it, this dog had what amounted to an antipathy toward me; really. And, I wondered if I mightn't overcome this antipathy. So, I tried it for five more days, but it was always the same: snarl, sniff; move; faster; stare; gobble; RAAGGGHHH; smile; snarl; BAM. Well, now; by this time Columbus Avenue was strewn with hamburger rolls and I was less offended than disgusted. So I decided to kill the dog.

(PETER *raises his hand in protest.*)

Oh, don't be so alarmed, Peter; I didn't succeed. The day I tried to kill the dog I bought only one hamburger and what I thought was a murderous portion of rat poison. When I bought the hamburger I asked the man not to bother with the rolls, all I wanted was the meat. I expected some reaction from him, like: We don't sell no hamburgers without rolls; or, wha' d'ya wanna do,

eat it out'a ya han's? But no; he smiled benignly, wrapped the
hamburger in waxed paper, and said: A bite for ya pussycat? I
wanted to say: No, not really; it's part of a plan to poison a dog
I know. But, you can't say "a dog I know" without sounding
funny; so I said, a little too loud, I'm afraid, and too formally:
YES, A BITE FOR MY PUSSYCAT. People looked up. It
always happens when I try to simplify things; people look up.
But that's neither hither nor thither. So. On my way back to the
rooming-house, I kneaded the hamburger and the rat poison
together between my hands, at that point feeling as much sadness as disgust. I opened the door to the entrance hall, and
there the monster was, waiting to take the offering and then
jump me. Poor bastard; he never did learn that the moment he
took to smile before he went for me gave me time enough to get
out of range. BUT, there he was; malevolence with an erection,
waiting. I put the poison patty down, moved toward the stairs
and watched. The poor animal gobbled the food down as usual,
smiled, which made me almost sick, and then, BAM. But, I
sprinted up the stairs, as usual, and the dog didn't get me, as
usual. AND IT CAME TO PASS THAT THE BEAST WAS
DEATHLY ILL. I knew this because he no longer attended me,
and because the landlady sobered up. She stopped me in the
hall the same evening of the attempted murder and confided
the information that God had struck her puppy-dog a surely
fatal blow. She had forgotten her bewildered lust, and her eyes
were wide open for the first time. They looked like the dog's
eyes. She sniveled and implored me to pray for the animal. I
wanted to say to her: Madam, I have myself to pray for, the
black queen, the Puerto Rican family, the person in the front
room whom I've never seen, the woman who cries deliberately
behind her closed door, and the rest of the people in all rooming-houses, everywhere; besides, Madam, I don't understand
how to pray. But . . . to simplify things . . . I told her I would
pray. She looked up. She said that I was a liar and that I probably wanted the dog to die. I told her, and there was so much

truth here, that I didn't want the dog to die. I didn't, and not just because I'd poisoned him. I'm afraid that I must tell you I wanted the dog to live so that I could see what our new relationship might come to.

(PETER *indicates his increasing displeasure and slowly growing antagonism.*)

Please understand, Peter; that sort of thing *is* important. We have to know the effect of our actions.

(*Another deep sigh.*)

Well, anyway; the dog recovered. I have no idea why, unless he was a descendant of the puppy that guarded the gates of hell or some such resort. I'm not up on my mythology.

(*He pronounces the word myth-o-*logy.)

Are you?

(PETER *sets to thinking, but* JERRY *goes on.*)

At any rate, and you've missed the eight-thousand-dollar question, Peter; at any rate, the dog recovered his health and the landlady recovered her thirst, in no way altered by the bow-wow's deliverance. When I came home from a movie that was playing on Forty-second Street, a movie I'd seen, or one that was very much like one or several I'd seen, after the landlady told me puppykins was better, I was so hoping for the dog to be waiting for me. I was . . . well, how would you put it . . . enticed? . . . fascinated? . . . no, I don't think so . . . heart-shatteringly anxious, that's it; I was heart-shatteringly anxious to confront my friend again.

(PETER *reacts scoffingly.*)

Yes, Peter; friend. That's the only word for it. I was heart-shatteringly et cetera to confront my doggy friend again. I came in the door and advanced, unafraid, to the center of the entrance hall. The beast was there . . . looking at me. And, you know, he looked better for his scrape with the nevermind. I stopped; I looked at him; he looked at me. I think . . . I think we stayed a

long time that way . . . still, stone-statue . . . just looking at one
another. I looked more into his face than he looked into mine. I
mean, I can concentrate longer at looking into a dog's face than
a dog can look into mine, or into anybody else's face for that
matter. But during that twenty seconds or two hours that we
looked into each other's face, we made contact. Now, here is
what I had wanted to happen: I loved the dog now, and I wanted him to love me. I had tried to love, and I had tried to kill, and
both had been unsuccessful by themselves. I hoped . . . and I
don't really know why I expected the dog to understand anything, much less my motivations . . . I hoped that the dog would
understand.

    (PETER *seems to be hypnotized.*)

   It's just . . . it's just that . . .

    (JERRY *is abnormally tense now.*)

. . . it's just that if you can't deal with people, you have to make
a start somewhere. WITH ANIMALS!

    (*Much faster now, like a conspirator.*)

Don't you see? A person has to have some way of dealing with
SOMETHING! With a bed, with a cockroach, with a mirror . . .
no, that's too hard, that's one of the last steps. With a cockroach,
with a . . . with a . . . with a carpet, a roll of toilet paper . . . no,
not that, either . . . that's a mirror, too; always check bleeding.
You see how hard it is to find things? With a street corner . . .
with a wisp of smoke, a wisp . . . of smoke . . . with . . . with
pornographic playing cards, with a strongbox . . . WITHOUT A
LOCK . . . with love, with vomiting, with crying, with fury because
the pretty little ladies aren't pretty little ladies, with making
money with your body which is an act of love and I could prove
it, with howling because you're alive; with God. WITH GOD
WHO IS A BLACK QUEEN WHO WEARS A KIMONO
AND PLUCKS HIS EYEBROWS, WHO IS A WOMAN
WHO CRIES WITH DETERMINATION BEHIND HER
CLOSED DOOR . . . with God who, I'm told, turned his back

on the whole thing some time ago . . . with . . . someday with people.

(JERRY *sighs the next word heavily.*)

People. With an idea; a concept. And where better, where ever better in this humiliating excuse for a jail, where better to communicate one single simpleminded idea than in an entrance hall? Where? It would be A START! Where better to make a beginning . . . to understand and just possibly be understood . . . a beginning of an understanding, than with . . .

(*Here* JERRY *seems to fall into almost grotesque fatigue.*)

. . . than with A DOG. Just that; a dog.

(*Here there is a silence that might be prolonged for a moment or so; then* JERRY *wearily finishes his story.*)

A dog. It seemed like a perfectly sensible idea. Man is a dog's best friend, remember. So: The dog and I looked at each other. I longer than the dog. And what I saw then has been the same ever since. Whenever the dog and I see each other we both stop where we are. We regard each other with a mixture of sadness and suspicion, and then we feign indifference. We walk past each other safely; we have an understanding. It's very sad, but you'll have to admit that it is an understanding. We had made many attempts at contact, and we had failed. The dog has returned to garbage and I to solitary but free passage. I have not returned. I mean to say, I have *gained* solitary free passage, if that much further loss can be said to be gain. I have learned that neither kindness nor cruelty by themselves, independent of each other, creates any effect beyond themselves; and I have learned that the two combined, together, at the same time, are the teaching emotion. And what is gained is loss. And what has been the result: The dog and I have attained a compromise; more of a bargain, really. We neither love nor hurt because we do not try to reach each other. And, *was* trying to feed the dog an act of love? And, perhaps, was the dog's attempt to bite me *not* an act of love? If we can so misunderstand, well then, why have we invented the word love in the first place?

(*There is silence.*)

The Story of Jerry and the Dog: the end.

(PETER *is silent.*)

Well, Peter?

(JERRY *is suddenly cheerful.*)

Well, Peter? Do you think I could sell that story to the *Reader's Digest* and make a couple of hundred bucks for "The Most Unforgettable Character I've Ever Met"? Huh?

(JERRY *is animated, but* PETER *is disturbed.*)

Oh, come on, now, Peter; tell me what you think.

PETER *(Numb.)*

I . . . I don't understand . . . I don't think I . . .

(*Now, almost tearfully.*)

Why did you tell me all of this?

JERRY

Why not?

PETER

I DON'T UNDERSTAND!

JERRY

(*Furious; but whispering.*)

That's a lie.

PETER

No. No, it's not.

JERRY *(Quietly.)*

I tried to explain it to you as I went along. I went slowly; it all has to do with . . .

PETER

I DON'T WANT TO HEAR ANYMORE. I don't understand you, or your landlady, or her dog . . .

JERRY

Her dog! I thought it was my . . . No. No, you're right. It *is* her dog.

    (Looks at PETER, *intently, shaking his head.)*

I don't know what I was thinking about; of course you don't understand.

    (In a monotone, wearily.)

I don't live in your block; I'm not married to two parakeets, or whatever your setup is. I am a *permanent transient,* and my home is the sickening rooming-houses on the West Side of New York City, which is the greatest city in the world. Amen. And I'm here, and I'm not leaving.

PETER *(Consulting his watch.)*

Well, you may not be, but I must be getting home soon.

JERRY

Oh, come on; stay a little while longer.

PETER

I really should get home; you see . . .

JERRY

    (Tickles PETER's *ribs with his fingers.)*

Oh, come on.

PETER

    (He is very ticklish; as JERRY *continues to tickle him his voice becomes falsetto.)*

No, I . . . OHHHHH! Don't do that. Stop, stop. Ohhh, no, no.

JERRY

Oh, come on.

PETER *(As* JERRY *tickles.)*

Oh, hee, hee, hee. I must go. I . . . hee, hee, hee. After all, the parakeets will be getting dinner ready soon. Hee, hee. And the cats are setting the table. Stop, stop, and, and . . .

(PETER *is beside himself now.*)
. . . and we're having . . . hee, hee . . . uh . . . ho, ho, ho
(JERRY *stops tickling* PETER, *but the combination of
the tickling and his own mad whimsy has* PETER
*laughing almost hysterically. As his laughter con-
tinues, then subsides,* JERRY *watches him, with a
curious fixed smile.*)

JERRY

Peter?

PETER

Oh, ha, ha, ha, ha, ha. What? What?

JERRY

Listen, now.

PETER

Oh ho, ho. What . . . what is it, Jerry? Oh, my.

JERRY (*Mysteriously.*)
Peter, do you want to know what happened at the zoo?

PETER

Ah, ha, ha. The what? Oh, yes; the zoo. Oh, ho, ho. Well, I had
my own zoo there for a moment with . . . hee, hee, the parakeets
getting dinner ready, and the . . . ha, ha, whatever it was, the . . .

JERRY (*Calmly.*)
Yes, that was very funny, Peter. I wouldn't have expected it. But
do you want to hear about what happened at the zoo, or not?

PETER

Yes. Yes, by all means; tell me what happened at the zoo. Oh,
my. I don't know what happened to me.

JERRY

Now I'll let you in on what happened at the zoo; but first, I should tell you why I went to the zoo. I went to the zoo to find out more about the way people exist with animals, and the way animals exist with each other, and with people too. It probably wasn't a fair test, what with everyone separated by bars from everyone else, the animals for the most part from each other, and always the people from the animals. But, if it's a zoo, that's the way it is.

(*He pokes* PETER *on the arm.*)

Move over.

PETER (*Friendly.*)

I'm sorry, haven't you enough room?

(*He shifts a little.*)

JERRY (*Smiling slightly.*)

Well, all the animals are there, and all the people are there, and it's Sunday, and all the children are there.

(*He pokes* PETER *again.*)

Move over.

PETER (*Patiently, still friendly.*)

All right.

(*He moves some more, and* JERRY *has all the room he might need.*)

JERRY

And it's a hot day, so all the stench is there, too, and all the balloon sellers, and all the ice cream sellers, and all the seals are barking, and all the birds are screaming.

(*Pokes* PETER *harder.*)

Move over!

PETER (*Beginning to be annoyed.*)

Look here, you have more than enough room!

(*But he moves more and is now fairly cramped at one end of the bench.*)

JERRY

And I am there, and it's feeding time at the lions' house, and the lion keeper comes into the lion cage, one of the lion cages, to feed one of the lions.

(Punches PETER *on the arm, hard.)*

MOVE OVER!

PETER *(Very annoyed.)*

I can't move over any more, and stop hitting me. What's the matter with you?

JERRY

Do you want to hear the story?

(Punches PETER's *arm again.)*

PETER *(Flabbergasted.)*

I'm not so sure! I certainly don't want to be punched in the arm.

JERRY *(Punches* PETER's *arm again.)*

Like that?

PETER

Stop it! What's the matter with you?

JERRY

I'm crazy, you bastard.

PETER

That isn't funny.

JERRY

Listen to me, Peter. I want this bench. You go sit on the bench over there, and if you're good I'll tell you the rest of the story.

PETER *(Flustered.)*

But . . . whatever for? What *is* the matter with you? Besides, I see no reason why I should give up this bench. I sit on this bench almost every Sunday afternoon, in good weather. It's secluded here; there's never anyone sitting here, so I have it all to myself.

JERRY *(Softly.)*

Get off this bench, Peter; I want it.

PETER *(Almost whining.)*

No.

JERRY

I said I want this bench, and I'm going to have it. Now get over there.

PETER

People can't have everything they want. You should know that; it's a rule; people can have some of the things they want, but they can't have everything.

JERRY *(Laughs.)*

Imbecile! You're slow-witted.

PETER

Stop that!

JERRY

You're a vegetable! Go lie down on the ground.

PETER *(Intense.)*

Now *you* listen to me. I've put up with you all afternoon.

JERRY

Not really.

PETER

LONG ENOUGH. I've put up with you long enough. I've listened to you because you seemed . . . well, because I thought you wanted to talk to somebody.

JERRY

You put things well; economically, and, yet . . . oh, what is the word I want to put justice to your . . . JESUS, you make me sick . . . get off here and give me my bench.

PETER

MY BENCH!

JERRY *(Pushes* PETER *off the bench.)*

Get out of my sight.

PETER *(Regaining his position.)*

God da . . . mn you. That's enough! I've had enough of you. I will not give up this bench; you can't have it, and that's that. Now, go away.

*(*JERRY *snorts but does not move.)*

Go away, I said.

*(*JERRY *does not move.)*

Get away from here. If you don't move on . . . you're a bum . . . that's what you are . . . If you don't move on, I'll get a policeman here and make you go.

*(*JERRY *laughs, stays.)*

I warn you, I'll call a policeman.

JERRY *(Softly.)*

You won't find a policeman around here; they're all over on the west side of the park chasing fairies down from trees or out of the bushes. That's all they do. That's their function. So scream your head off; it won't do you any good.

PETER

POLICE! I warn you, I'll have you arrested. POLICE!

(Pause.)

I said POLICE!

(Pause.)

I feel ridiculous.

JERRY

You look ridiculous: a grown man screaming for the police on a bright Sunday afternoon in the park with nobody harming you. If a policeman *did* fill his quota and come sludging over this way he'd probably take you in as a nut.

PETER (*With disgust and impotence.*)
Great God, I just came here to read, and now you want me to give up the bench. You're mad.

JERRY
Hey, I got news for you, as they say. I'm on your precious bench, and you're never going to have it for yourself again.

PETER (*Furious.*)
Look, you; get off my bench. I don't care if it makes any sense or not. I want this bench to myself; I want you OFF IT!

JERRY (*Mocking.*)
Aw . . . look who's mad.

PETER
GET OUT!

JERRY
No.

PETER
I WARN YOU!

JERRY
Do you know how ridiculous you look *now?*

PETER
(*His fury and self-consciousness have possessed him.*)
It doesn't matter.
(*He is almost crying.*)
GET AWAY FROM MY BENCH!

JERRY
Why? You have everything in the world you want; you've told me about your home, and your family, and *your own* little zoo. You have everything, and now you want this bench. Are these the things men fight for? Tell me, Peter, is this bench, this iron

and this wood, is this your honor? Is this the thing in the world you'd fight for? Can you think of anything more absurd?

PETER

Absurd? Look, I'm not going to talk to you about honor, or even try to explain it to you. Besides, it isn't a question of honor; but even if it were, you wouldn't understand.

JERRY *(Contemptuously.)*

You don't even know what you're saying, do you? This is probably the first time in your life you've had anything more trying to face than changing yours cats' toilet box. Stupid! Don't you have any idea, not even the slightest, what other people *need?*

PETER

Oh, boy, listen to you; well, you don't need this bench. That's for sure.

JERRY

Yes; yes, I do.

PETER *(Quivering.)*

I've come here for years; I have hours of great pleasure, great satisfaction, right here. And that's important to a man. I'm a responsible person, and I'm a GROWNUP. This is my bench, and you have no right to take it away from me.

JERRY

Fight for it, then. Defend yourself; defend your bench.

PETER

You've *pushed* me to it. Get up and fight.

JERRY

Like a man?

PETER *(Still angry.)*

Yes, like a man, if you insist on mocking me even further.

JERRY

I'll have to give you credit for one thing: You *are* a vegetable, and a slightly nearsighted one, I think . . .

PETER

THAT'S ENOUGH . . .

JERRY

. . . but, you know, as they say on TV all the time—you know—and I mean this, Peter, you have a certain dignity; it surprises me . . .

PETER

STOP!

JERRY *(Rises lazily.)*

Very well, Peter, we'll battle for the bench, but we're not evenly matched.

(He takes out and clicks open an ugly-looking knife.)

PETER

(Suddenly awakening to the reality of the situation.)

You are mad! You're stark raving mad! YOU'RE GOING TO KILL ME?

(But before PETER *has time to think what to do,* JERRY *tosses the knife at* PETER's *feet.)*

JERRY

There you go. Pick it up. You have the knife and we'll be more evenly matched.

PETER *(Horrified.)*

No!

JERRY

(Rushes over to PETER, *grabs him by the collar;* PETER *rises; their faces almost touch.)*

Now you pick up that knife, and you fight with me. You fight for your self-respect; you fight for that goddamned bench.

PETER *(Struggling.)*
No! Let . . . go of me! He . . . Help!

JERRY *(Slaps* PETER *on each "fight.")*
You fight, you miserable bastard; fight for that bench; fight for your manhood, you pathetic little vegetable.
(Spits in PETER's *face.)*
You couldn't even get your wife with a male child.

PETER *(Breaks away, enraged.)*
It's a matter of genetics, not manhood, you . . . you monster.
(He darts down, picks up the knife and backs off a little; he is breathing heavily.)
I'll give you one last chance; get out of here and leave me alone!
(He holds the knife with a firm arm, but far in front of him, not to attack but to defend.)

JERRY *(Sighs heavily.)*
So be it!
(With a rush, he charges PETER *and impales himself completely on the knife. Tableau: For just a moment, complete silence,* JERRY *impaled on the knife at the end of* PETER's *still firm arm. Then* PETER *screams, pulls away, leaving the knife in* JERRY. JERRY *is motionless, on point. Then he, too, screams, and it must be the sound of an infuriated and fatally wounded animal. With the knife in him, he stumbles back to the bench that* PETER *had vacated. He crumbles there, sitting, facing* PETER, *his eyes wide in agony, his mouth open.)*

PETER *(Whispering.)*
Oh my God, oh my God, oh my God . . .
(He repeats these words many times, very rapidly. JERRY *is dying; but now his expression seems to change. His features relax, and while his voice*

varies, sometimes wrenched with pain, for the most
part he seems removed from his dying. He smiles.)

JERRY

Peter, thank you, Peter. I mean that, now; thank you very much.

(PETER's *mouth drops open. He cannot move; he is*
transfixed.)

I came unto you

(He laughs, so faintly.)

and you have comforted me. Dear Peter.

PETER *(Almost fainting.)*

Oh my God!

JERRY

You'd better go now. Somebody might come by, and you don't
want to be here when anyone comes.

PETER

(Does not move, but begins to weep.)

Oh my God, oh my God.

JERRY

And Peter, I'll tell you something now; you're not really a vegetable; it's all right, you're an animal. You're an animal, too. But
you'd better hurry now, Peter. Hurry, you'd better go . . .

(JERRY *takes a handkerchief and with great effort and*
pain wipes the knife handle clean of fingerprints.)

Hurry away, Peter.

(PETER *begins to stagger away.)*

Wait . . . wait, Peter. Take your book . . . book. Right here . . .
beside me . . . on your bench . . . my bench, rather. Come . . .
take your book.

(PETER *starts for the book, but retreats.)*

Hurry . . . Peter.

(PETER *rushes to the bench, grabs the book, retreats.*)
Very good, Peter . . . very good. Now . . . hurry away.
  (PETER *hesitates for a moment, then flees, stage left.*)
Hurry away . . .
  (*His eyes are closed now.*)

PETER

OH MY GOD!

JERRY

Hurry away, your parakeets are making the dinner . . . the cats . . .
are setting the table . . .

PETER (*Offstage. A pitiful howl.*)

OH MY GOD!

JERRY

  (*His eyes still closed, he shakes his head and speaks; a
  combination of scornful mimicry and supplication.*)
Oh . . . my . . . God.
  (*He is dead.*)

END OF PLAY

ALSO BY EDWARD ALBEE
AVAILABLE FROM THE OVERLOOK PRESS

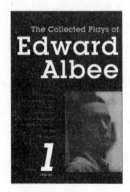

The Collected Plays of Edward Albee

Volume 1 (1958–1965) ☒978-1-58567-884-6 ☒$25.95
Volume 2 (1966–1977) ☒978-1-59020-053-7 ☒$25.95
Volume 3 (1978–2003) ☒978-1-59020-114-5 ☒$25.95

"A major playwright who helped to change
the shape of contemporary drama here and abroad."
—Vincent Canby, *The New York Times*

"Albee throws the abyss in our faces with exhilarating,
articulate, daring and dark, grown-up dazzle."
—*Chicago Tribune*

"One of the few genuinely great living American dramatists."
—Ben Brantley, *The New York Times*

THE OVERLOOK PRESS
New York
www.overlookpress.com